CW01303005

MARIE CORELLI:

Shakespeare's Champion

MARIE CORELLI: Shakespeare's Champion

Jann Tracy

Walking Stork Publications

First published in 2017 by Walking Stork Publications

Copyright ©Jann Tracy 2017

The right of Jann Tracy to be identified as the author of this work has been asserted by her in accordance with the Copyright, Designs and Patents Act 1988

ISBN 978-1-9997979-1-1

Cover image © Shakespeare Birthplace Trust

All other images © Shakespeare Birthplace Trust except those below

Faucit Memorial © Jann Tracy
Marie Corelli Memorial Grave © Ellie Stevenson

Cover Design by designforwriters.com

Marie Corelli on board Tommy Lipton's yacht
With Tommy Lipton and Edward Morris

CONTENTS

Introduction   1

CHAPTERS

1. At First   7
2. Faucit Memorial   13
3. Bancroft Basin   19
4. Henley Street   23
5. Harvard House   35
6. Conservation   43
7. Festivities   51
8. Wartime   55
9. Reputation   65
10. Death and Afterwards   81

Conclusion   85

APPENDICES

A. Early Life: the years before Stratford   91
B. Timeline   103
C. Changes to Henley Street   113
D. Hall's Croft   115
E. Love and Marie Corelli   119
F. Loyalist and Others   125
G. Map: places of interest   131

ILLUSTRATIONS

Front cover: Marie Corelli at the wheel
Marie Corelli on Tommy Lipton's yacht
Frontispiece from *Treasures of Heaven*
Mason Croft, Marie Corelli's home
Faucit Memorial in the Swan Theatre
Bancroft Basin with Pool
Cottages and Birch's China Shop, 1902
Two cottages being Demolished, 1904
Harvard House Steering Committee
The Firs on Rother Street, c1960
Tudor House with Stucco, 1902-03
Alveston Leys Fete, c1916
The Sketch
Tennis at Mason Croft, c1922
Marie Corelli's Funeral Cortege, 1924
Marie Corelli in her conservatory
Ponies, Trap and Marie Corelli
Marie Corelli Memorial Grave, 2017

ACKNOWLEDGEMENTS
SOURCES AND BACKGROUND READING
INDEX

Frontispiece from *Treasures of Heaven*

INTRODUCTION

No-one writes or mentions Marie Corelli much anymore, and this book is designed to fill that gap. It is neither extensive, nor comprehensive and is meant only to give a flavour of the person who was so supremely successful in the face of overwhelming odds.

Marie Corelli was one of Stratford-upon-Avon's most flamboyant and contentious personalities. If you've never heard of her, she was the best-selling author of her day, outselling Charles Dickens, HG Wells and Wilkie Collins combined. Queen Victoria was a fan and insisted on being sent a copy of each new book. Marie was so famous in the United States it was proposed that a city in Colorado be named after her. She also had a rose named after her, it was a fragrant, salmon pink hybrid perpetual, sadly no longer obtainable.

Jann Tracy

Marie was a conservationist before anyone knew what that was. She was a passionate lover of the works of William Shakespeare and thought the town of Stratford-upon-Avon ought to reflect his Tudor heritage.

After a brief romance with Stratford, when she was seen solely as a Lady Bountiful, she came into conflict with the town's male worthies who had long ruled, virtually unopposed, and who resented her headlong approach to change. She was determined that this small market town should cherish and reflect its most famous son.

What follows are some of the hassles and tussles she was embroiled in.

Mason Croft: Marie Corelli's home

CHAPTERS

CHAPTER 1
AT FIRST

Marie Corelli first visited the sleepy little country town of Stratford-upon-Avon in May 1890. She was accompanied by her half-brother Eric Mackay and her great friend Bertha Vyver and they stayed at the Falcon Hotel. Nine years later she came to stay for good and the town hasn't been the same since.

When Marie and Bertha came back to Stratford in 1899, Marie leased Hall's Croft from Mrs Catherine Croker for six months. While there she entertained Sarah Bernhardt and they made the pilgrimage to Shakespeare's grave together. Marie wanted to buy Hall's Croft, but Mrs Croker moved back in, so Marie and Bertha moved down the road to the Dower House. You can see the location of these properties on the map in the appendices.

Jann Tracy

In 1872 the vicar of Holy Trinity Church, Dr John Day Collis, bought a large property at the corner of Church Street and Old Town and established Trinity College. Three years later he bought the property next door to be used for teaching, this had originally been two, possibly timber-framed, 16th century or earlier, houses, called Mason Croft. At the beginning of 1901, both Mason Croft and the College were owned by JC Tregarthen and Marie took out an 18 month lease on the house, with an option to purchase. The house was a neglected property in need of repair and took some considerable effort to make it habitable, but at the beginning of 1901 Marie and Bertha moved in.

Trinity College closed in 1904, after which it was used as an army school and was a leading preparatory school for Woolwich and Sandhurst military colleges. When the school moved to Maidenhead in 1908, it was renamed The Royal Army School. Marie bought the college building, and the annexe, which had been the dining hall of the college, was remodelled as her music room.

Photographs show Mason Croft, during Marie's residency, with railings at the front, a portico over the entrance, Virginia Creeper on the walls, and flower-packed window boxes. The iron railings were requisitioned towards the end of the First World War, along with most of the others in town, to help the war effort. After the Second World War the British Council moved in and all Marie's additions to the frontage were removed. The building is now the Shakespeare Institute, part of the University of Birmingham.

In 1899, while still living at the Dower House, Marie started what was to be her charitable contribution to the town by paying for the whole Grammar School to go to the circus, and in December the same year, she spoke to over 1,000 people at a PSA (pleasant Sunday afternoon) gathering in Leamington Spa, when she also distributed prizes.

On 1 January 1900, 1,000 Stratford-upon-Avon National Schools children were invited by Marie to a party at the Shakespeare Memorial Theatre, followed on 6th and 12th by parties for 500 needy Birmingham children and 270 Stratford Infants School children. In July she paid for over 600 National Schools children to visit Rugby Park.

Jann Tracy

Following on from these outings, in October 1900 George Boyden, editor of the *Stratford-upon-Avon Herald* revealed in the paper:

> that the popular novelist is still in Stratford, and that she is likely to remain here. This is an announcement that we make with a good deal of pleasure, inasmuch as Stratford cannot afford to lose one who has filled the role of Lady Bountiful so admirably.

As Teresa Ransom says in her book, *The Mysterious Miss Marie Corelli: Queen of Victorian Bestsellers*: 'She needed to become part of the community, and now that she had money, she wanted to use it for the benefit of others.' There are numerous other examples of her generosity, of which these are a small sample.

Marie was musical and had once contemplated a career as a concert pianist and in 1901 she was invited to become President of the Stratford-upon-Avon Choral Union, subsequently organising a sell-out concert at the Shakespeare Memorial Theatre starring, amongst others, Dame Clara Butt. All the guest artists stayed at Mason Croft. In July she organised a concert on the river with illuminated boats. In a letter to the young actor and personal friend Halliwell Hobbes, she wrote that 'it was such a pretty sight.' Marie was determined to make her mark.

In January 1902 she was invited to be the guest of honour of the Mayor of Birmingham, when she gave a talk on literature to a packed hall. She spoke for an hour and the *Stratford-upon-Avon Herald* reported that, 'For a woman to entertain an audience for over an hour with a lecture on Literature is itself a remarkable feat... with scarcely a reference to notes, then it becomes... perhaps unique.'

Marie though was a complex figure, she loved to be generous and she also loved to be the centre of attention. In November 1902 two Shetland ponies (Puck & Ariel) and a carriage were delivered to Mason Croft from Scotland. Marie and Bertha began to take a carriage drive at the same time each day to the delight of crowds of adoring fans.

Trouble, however, was looming in the form of a debt and a memorial, both centred on Holy Trinity Church.

CHAPTER 2
FAUCIT MEMORIAL

In October 1900 Marie heard there was a large debt of £900 (over £100,000 now) owed by Holy Trinity Church and, eager to help, tried to raise funds to pay it off. She wasn't the only one.

Sir Theodore Martin had previously given a green marble pulpit to the church in memory of his late wife, actress Helen Faucit (1817-98), showing her portrait as Saint Helena. It can be seen today in the church, to the right of the front row of pews.

At the Inaugural Festival for the new Shakespeare Memorial Theatre, 23 April 1879, Helen Faucit, a noted actress of her generation, had been persuaded to come out of retirement, aged 51, to play Beatrice in the production of *Much Ado about Nothing*, which was the first play on the new stage.

Sir Theodore now wanted to erect a large bas-relief memorial to her in the chancel, opposite the Shakespeare bust. This was a replica of the one he had placed in the chancel of the church at Llantysilio (near the couple's country house) which was itself a reproduction of one exhibited by John Henry Foley at the Royal Academy in 1856. Sir Theodore also offered to pay the church's debt.

Marie, in her turn, offered the then vicar, George Arbuthnot, a cheque for £900 to pay off the church's debt immediately if the erecting of the memorial was stopped. He told her that unfortunately the Bishop of Worcester had already approved the memorial and it would therefore go ahead. She subsequently discovered that the installation of the Faucit memorial meant taking down existing memorials, including one to a previous vicar whose widow had not been informed and whose permission had not been obtained.

Armed with this knowledge and her determination to preserve the shrine to Shakespeare, Marie wrote to over 15 national newspapers, setting off a hue and cry over the desecration of Shakespeare's grave. In her

Marie Corelli: Shakespeare's Champion

initial letter of 22 October 1900 she wrote of: 'a shrine of unbroken peace and sanctity.' In contrast the *Birmingham Gazette* of 26 October stated that: 'the chancel is crowded with the tombs, statuettes, brasses, slabs and memorials of others.'

Most papers, however were on her side, including *The Star* of London which stated that: 'Miss Marie Corelli's protest against the placing of the bust there evidently has support.' The *Stratford-upon-Avon Herald*'s editorial of 26 October was also in her favour, and the *Whitehall Review* of 27 October, whilst referring to her as 'the tempestuous Marie' agreed with her point of view. The *Birmingham Post* also supported her: 'Miss Marie Corelli deserves hearty thanks for courageously and promptly protesting against this proposed "second" Faucit Memorial.'

She took the case to the Court of Arches, which is the highest court in the Church of England, being the court of appeal of the Archbishop of Canterbury, and won.

Eventually, in December 1900, the Faucit Memorial was erected in the Shakespeare Memorial Theatre. It is today in the stairwell of the Ferguson Room in the Swan Theatre, as shown in the photograph.

Sir Sidney Lee, then editor of the *Dictionary of National Biography*, later Chairman of the Shakespeare Birthplace Trust (SBT), sometimes her foe, but also a friend, wrote to her:

> No one can be in any doubt that it was your own energetic intervention which caused the satisfactory solution of the difficulty... Most of the London papers... with perfect rightness, consider that you have saved a national monument from a serious peril. The victory is certainly yours.

The success of using her fame to awaken the public's interest in causes involving Shakespeare's name and reputation may have set a precedent for her future behaviour. Sadly, universal approval wasn't always forthcoming, despite her next target being an action by the town council which deprived the townsfolk of a much enjoyed facility, the Bancroft Basin.

Faucit Memorial in the Swan Theatre
(photography by Jann Tracy)

Bancroft Basin with Pool

CHAPTER 3
BANCROFT BASIN

The Bancroft was originally an area of land where the townspeople grazed their animals. In 1816 when the canal opened, the area was turned into a basin for boats which had travelled down the canal from Birmingham, and ultimately became surrounded by wharves and warehouses and businesses related to trade brought by the boats.

A second basin was built in 1826, in what had been the end of the Stratford to Birmingham canal. When railways became the transport of choice, the land around the basins became owned by various railway companies, the boating trade diminished and the area became a bit of an eyesore.

The Memorial Theatre opened in 1879 and was originally further away from the area now known as Bancroft Gardens. The second canal basin on the Bancroft was cleared and turned into a large ornamental pond to form part of new formal riverside gardens, as shown in the photograph of 1900. Children used to swim in this shallow lake, and it was a popular town attraction. The town council however, decided that it was a potential danger to children and had it drained, leaving a smelly pool that became a potential health hazard.

Although by then it was too late, in September 1901, Marie wrote to the *Stratford-upon-Avon Herald* regarding the draining of the basin which had left behind stagnant mud possibly harbouring several unpleasant diseases. Whether she intended the basin to become a pond again, or merely wanted to make a point, is not known and in *The Avon Star: A literary manual for the Stratford-on-Avon season of 1903, April 23rd*, she described the area as having been 'one of the prettiest bits in Stratford.'

As to the accusation that the pond was smelly, Marie said not, that it was just somebody who had been misled by their 'over-excitable nose' imagining that the basin 'emitted an undesirable perfume' but in fact the nose was wrong. Ironically however, since the 'unfortunate and innocent piece of water' had been 'ruthlessly drained out and filled up, it [had] revenged itself by becoming a perfect distillery of objectionable odours.' The council though had its way and instead of refilling the Basin with water filled it in with earth.

The Avon soon began to attract those who wanted a day away from Victorian industrial towns, and go boating for pleasure. Boathouses and pleasure boat piers opened up and down the Avon to serve the new day trippers and tourists.

Marie hadn't won the battle this time, but the next tussle would resonate far beyond the town's boundaries, when an American industrialist decided to give Stratfordians a library.

Cottages and Birch's China Shop, 1902

CHAPTER 4
HENLEY STREET

> I... strongly reaffirm my indictment against the neglect of literary England to guard and preserve what few genuine relics of Shakespeare she still possesses.

So wrote Marie in a chapter entitled 'The Body-Snatchers' in her book, *The Plain Truth of the Stratford-on-Avon Controversy concerning the fully-intended demolition of old houses in Henley Street, and the changes proposed to be effected on the National Ground of Shakespeare's Birthplace* [1903].

Using her by now finely honed letter-writing-in-protest skills, Marie entered the arena of the Henley Street Controversy, which could be regarded as the first local conservation campaign. It had started at the end of 1902, eventually creating warring factions in town and a bitter fight between the town council (commercialism) and Marie (conservationism).

Andrew Carnegie had been asked to donate a free library to Stratford-upon-Avon and after the town passed his 'Schedule of Questions' two sites were chosen: Henley Street, near the Birthplace and the Market Hall (favoured by Marie). Famous actress Ellen Terry also suggested a site near the theatre. However, Henley Street was chosen. Four old cottages along with Birch's china shop, built in 1563, were to be demolished to make way for the new building. The Birch family had run a china and glass shop on the site since at least 1883.

Carnegie was born in Dunfermline, Scotland in 1835 and emigrated with his parents to the United States in 1848. He made a fortune in the steel industry and became a great philanthropist. He opened his first free library in Dunfermline in 1883, and the third in his adopted home town of Allegheny, Pittsburgh, in 1890. Eventually, over 2000 free libraries carrying his name, were opened worldwide between 1883 and 1929.

Marie Corelli: Shakespeare's Champion

A *New York Times* article from 1903, titled 'Carnegie and Corelli', stated that while most towns were very grateful to receive a grant, Carnegie's project was not without controversy. For example, some people objected to the way in which he'd made his money. In the case of Stratford-upon-Avon there were objections to the proposed building for conservation reasons, and according to the paper 'this resulted in a library which blends into the half-timbered neighbouring buildings.'

Marie was at first reluctant to be involved, due to a dispute with *The Gentlewoman* magazine, which had accused her of blatant self-publicity, and in December 1902 when she received a letter from Lady Colin Campbell asking her to help save the old cottages, Marie refused as she didn't want further acrimony between herself and the town council. However, people continued asking her to intervene and in February 1903 she wrote to the *Morning Post* protesting against the proposed demolition of part of 'this unique old town.'

Ellen Terry then also wrote to the *Morning Post* in support of Marie, and *Vanity Fair* supported them both. Letters of protest against the proposal were received from around the world and printed in various newspapers. She was also supported by other notable people and organisations such as the British Archaeological Association, the British Museum, and Lord Warwick, and thus the decision to establish a free library in the town became a bitter contest between the Town Council and the 'Outsiders.' Just the scenario that Marie had hoped to avoid.

Allen S Walker, honorary correspondent of the British Archaeological Association informed the warring factions that he found 'ample cause for the intervention of antiquarian bodies.' He went on to explain that three of the five cottages contained sixteenth century timbers and that these three houses had been discovered to have belonged to relatives of Shakespeare. Two cottages (the property of the SBT Trustees) had been held by the husband of Shakespeare's grand-daughter, and the third cottage held by Shakespeare's cousin, sometime Town Clerk of Stratford on Avon. This latter was Birch's china shop and Walker recommended that its condition be interfered with as little as possible, and that the removal of the brick front should not be carried out for this and the cottages.

In a report of June 1903 to the Committee of the Society for the Protection of Ancient Buildings, two members of the committee wrote:

> We consider that the old houses... were well worthy of careful preservation from their intrinsic interest and age... a new front must be erected, and we consider that the whole of the ancient work which remains can be... retained unaltered... the new front should be constructed of timber.

They also suggested that the ground floor should be infilled with old brick, and that the upper storey should overhang the lower.

A sample of the tone used by most of the papers is to be found in the *Sunday Sun* of 17 May 1903:

Corelli v Stratford. An Appeal to the Londoner.

> In some things the truest progressive is the reactionary. Miss Corelli is right in her fight against the grovelling and Philistine parochialism of the elected persons of Stratford-upon-Avon. She should be supported.

Marie went to see Carnegie in London, but he only cared about preserving the Birthplace, and not about any other of the town's buildings. As far as he was concerned the whole of Henley Street could be demolished, as long as the Birthplace remained untouched. It would have been quite a meeting, between these two stubborn and opinionated people. Whilst she was out of town, the council started, at five o'clock in the morning, to demolish the two cottages next to the china shop. They had to stop temporarily due to the outrage of the town's other inhabitants, but later finished the job.

Now, part of the contemplated demolition consisted of the Hornby cottages (originally two cottages that had been made into one) which had belonged to Shakespeare's granddaughter and the Hart family, and the deeds were at the time housed in the Birthplace, so the Trustees knew there was a Shakespeare connection. Nicholas Fogg suggests that 'the cottages had once belonged to Thomas Quiney and that an obscure by-law forbade the destruction of any property that had been owned by Shakespeare's family.'

An emergency meeting of the Executive Committee of the SBT Trustees was held and it was decided that due to the partial demolition of the cottages it had been revealed that the majority of the original and ancient timberwork remained in place. On 16 May the *Birmingham Daily Gazette* wrote that Andrew Carnegie's gift was of even greater value than had been thought at first, and 'Miss Corelli will derive some satisfaction from the knowledge that in a measure her strenuous efforts have met with success.'

It was eventually established beyond doubt that the remaining two cottages *had* belonged to Shakespeare's granddaughter Elizabeth, wife of Thomas Nash, and the Hart family (Shakespeare's sister was Joan Hart). Ironically, Mary Hornby's collection of doubtful

Shakespeare relics (including the chair in the inglenook which had had several incarnations) was once housed in the Birthplace, when she was the Custodian, now the Birthplace shop is housed in the Hornby Cottages.

Later, in a piece published on 29 August 1903, *The Speaker* put the matter to rest and declared that the proposed site in Henley Street was:

> a vulgar faded street chiefly in modern brick, in which Shakespeare's birth place has had the misfortune to stand. Four frankly ugly cottages [stood] alongside the shrine... They were disreputable and decaying... It is now settled that... all genuine old work... shall be preserved and worked into the new building.

If you stand opposite the library in Henley Street and look from right to left, you can see that the library is now housed in the:

- Technical School, (a modern building constructed in the late 19th century)
- a space previously occupied by a house that burnt down at the end of the 19th century, and
- Birch's china shop (where Greene, Shakespeare's cousin had lived).

You can see how the Technical School now adjoins the library building, and where brickwork exists in place of timber. Then look further left to the footpath and railed garden where the two cottages were demolished, between the library entrance and Hornby Cottages (the Birthplace Shop). If you look closely you can see that today's library entrance seems a bit too pristine to be really old.

In 2017 the library and register office were housed in the same building, which means that the old chimney breast and niche downstairs which were in the library and thus accessible, will be in the register office, which will limit their access. However, have a peek upstairs at the genuinely old oak beams in the ceiling of what was once the Reading Room. Happily the entrance to the register office will be through the door of the old Technical School, in use again after so many years.

Marie's next foray into restoration was due to the appeal to her of an old house that she walked past regularly. It was sorely neglected and cried out to her to rescue it.

Two Cottages being Demolished, 1904

Harvard House Steering Committee
Tommy Lipton, Marie Corelli, Rudolph Lehmann, Edward Morris

CHAPTER 5
HARVARD HOUSE

Accordingly, in 1905 Marie became interested in Harvard House, a 16th century property at 26 High Street previously known as 'The Ancient House'. Harvard House was built in 1596 by wealthy townsman Thomas Rogers, a butcher and corn and cattle merchant. Rogers served as Alderman for the Stratford Corporation alongside John Shakespeare, William's father, so it is not beyond the realms of wild possibility that the two families knew each other. Thomas's daughter Katherine married Robert Harvard in April 1605, in Stratford, subsequently moving to Southwark where their son John was born in 1607. John grew up in London and married Ann Sadler in 1636, emigrating to America the following year. John Harvard died young, but his name lives on in the American college he helped to found. According to its website:

> Harvard is the oldest institution of higher education in the United States, established in 1636... named after the College's first benefactor, the young minister John Harvard of Charlestown, who upon his death in 1638 left his library and half his estate to the institution.

Marie resolved to do something about the situation, but unfortunately was away when the property went on the market and she knew nothing about the sale. Returning home she found that the house had been withdrawn as the highest bid of £950 (over £93,000 now) was not thought to be sufficient. So she quietly 'set to work on ways and means for purchasing it by private treaty.'

The house was in dire need of renovation and she found support for its restoration from a rich American couple. In the summer of 1905, Marie and Bertha were on board Tommy Lipton's yacht, *Erin*, for the Cowes Regatta, and met Mr and Mrs Edward Morris of Chicago. He was a millionaire, having made his fortune in the meat-packing business. Marie told them about Harvard House, describing it as a run-down sixteenth-century property. To her delight, he agreed that she should buy it on his behalf and arrange restoration at his expense, supporting her idea of the house becoming a sign of friendship between Britain and America. Restoration was to take four years. The photograph shows a meeting of the Harvard House steering committee. The house was furnished with period pieces as explained in the *Harvard House Guide Book* and *Ward Lock's Red Guide* of 1962:

> Miss Corelli subsequently supervised the restoration and furnishing of the house. It contains some fine Elizabethan furniture, Jacobean pewter, and some fifteenth-century domestic glass; but as far as possible the atmosphere of a peaceful domestic dwelling has been preserved, rather than that of a show-place.

In October 1909, Harvard House was opened by the then American Ambassador, Whitelaw Reid, and officially handed over to the university. Marie arranged for a special train to travel from Marylebone to Stratford and back on a day return, bringing the ambassador and invited guests. After the opening ceremony the 300 guests sang, 'For she's a jolly good fellow' to Marie before walking along the road to a sumptuous feast in a marquee in the Mason Croft garden. Later, Marie was voted as Chair of the Harvard House Trust, and a guide book was authorised.

Unfortunately, however, the finances of the Harvard House Trust suffered losses, first due to the death of Edward Morris in November 1913, at the young age of 47, followed by the First World War (1914 to 1918), the death of Viscount Bryce (appointed trustee in place of Edward Morris) in 1922, and the death of Marie Corelli in 1924. GT Lapsley and Bertha Vyver were appointed Trustee and Chair respectively, but the guide book wasn't finally published until 1929.

Marie Corelli: Shakespeare's Champion

In her introduction, written in 1909 and included in the guide book 20 years later, Marie explains:

> For many years the old building was cruelly neglected... a pathetic object of decaying beauty in the High Street, vulgarised... browbeaten... its quaint windows seemed to blink like poor tired eyes, asking : "What is to become of me when I get older and still more shaky than I am?"

We now know that with the help of Edward Morris she bought it to save it from further ruin, and secured its future.

Also in the guide book is an account of the opening ceremony and the transcription of a talk given by the Master of Emmanuel College, Cambridge, in which he said that what is known 'with regard to John Harvard's life is small indeed.' He went on to quote:

> It is a remarkable thing that a man who earned no distinction in life, who spent little more than a year in

the United States and died of consumption at the age of thirty-one, should yet rank with the immortals.

After the opening the Mayor, John Priest, wrote a letter to Marie in which he congratulated her:

> on the great success of this afternoon's function. It was a noble and patriotic move... thank you, for the part you have played in securing... in perpetuity that grand old Elizabethan House... which is of great importance... a great ornament to the town.

A plaque inside the house, written and paid for by Tommy Lipton in 1913, states:

> This House having been rescued from demolition and its Restoration Designed and Consummated by Miss Marie Corelli was purchased by Edward Morris Esq of Chicago and

Marie Corelli: Shakespeare's Champion

presented to Harvard University 6th October 1909

Today the house is in the care of the SBT which has looked after the property on behalf of Harvard University since 1990. The house was opened to the public during the refurbishment of New Place, but has alas, once more had it doors closed, only to be opened on certain days. Marie's work on Harvard House was an amazing achievement, but is only one of many restoration projects she fostered. The next chapter gives some more examples of her conservation work.

The Firs on Rother Street, c1960

CHAPTER 6
CONSERVATION

The appearance in Stratford-upon-Avon of so much apparently Tudor architecture is in large part due to Marie's wish to have a town that displayed and made the most of its Shakespearian heritage. This she achieved through chivvying owners, and paying for the work to be done.

Marie was particularly incensed by the amount of stucco in the town, where there should be Tudor beams, and in her pamphlet *With Shakespeare in his Garden* she wrote of:

> ancient gabled houses, all of which are being gradually relieved of the disguising stucco in which they were dressed to suit the stiff taste of Queen Anne's reign, and now are

> being shown in all their old-world charm of Elizabethan architecture.

As evidence of this in 1903 she paid for the restoration of numbers 23-24 High Street. Known as the Tudor House, owned at the time by the printer AJ Stanley, it's on the corner of High Street and Ely Street. Originally faced with stucco, as can be seen in the photograph, an elaborately carved corner post was uncovered during some repair work, and as a result, Marie gave Stanley £200 (now nearly £20,000) towards the house's restoration and appearance today.

Around the time Harvard House was being saved for future generations, The Firs, a large house on Rother Street, was sold and the gardens saved from development. The Rev. George Arbuthnot, vicar of Holy Trinity church with whom Marie was friendly, lived with his wife in The Firs when Marie and Bertha first moved to Stratford, but the couple moved out in 1908. As can be seen from the photograph, it was a large and imposing building, demolished in the 1970s. A rather plain police station now stands in its place, but the garden belongs to the town, and contains an 18th century dovecot in one corner, and a plaque:

> *Welcome to the Firs Gardens*
>
> *This delightfully tranquil corner of Stratford was refurbished in 1990: a joint project between Town and District Councils. 'The Firs', a nearby house no longer in existence, lends the gardens its name. When it was sold in 1910, Marie Corelli, the famous novelist, bought the gardens to preserve them as an open space for the benefit of the town.*

In 1911 the town council had failed to sell a plot of land on the Birmingham Road, and turned it instead into allotments. In 1918 NC Joseph of Birmingham, aluminium castings manufacturer, bid for the land for a factory and was accepted. The factory was furiously opposed by the 60 allotment holders, who'd worked their plots for seven years, along with Marie, the vicar, the secretary of the SBT, the grammar school headmaster and many other local worthies.

Reminiscent of the Faucit controversy there were angry letters in the national press. Local architect Guy Pemberton said this would mean, 'A row of short furnace stacks, belching forth sulphurous and deadly fumes [and as the site was to the west of the town] the prevailing wind will waft this gently over everything and all of us.' However, at this time the Birmingham Road wasn't the most salubrious of places as there was already a chemical factory, the gasworks, Birch's Skin Yard, and the clay pit for the brickworks, where there was daily blasting.

In a letter to the *Morning Post*, Marie revealed plans for a chemical manure factory at Shottery: 'Caught between the sulphurous and deadly fumes of the casting foundry and the stench of the Shottery factory, Stratford would become a most unhealthy place to be.'

As has already been seen, however, Marie wasn't always successful in her protests and after NC Joseph himself had firmly stated that there wouldn't be any belching of fumes, as the factory wasn't a smelting works, the proposal was passed. An aerial photograph of 1947 shows a sprawling complex, which made saucepans, kettles and other kitchen appliances.

More positively in 1913 the Guild of Stratford was established (an organisation originally suggested by Marie in 1901) which mostly dealt with conservation issues and Marie was on the committee. In 1914 she was chivvying the Guild to do something about the large number of trees being sold at Loxley and Welford, and these were subsequently saved from destruction.

She was also concerned with the 'wanton defacement of the Waterside cottages.' I think this involved some demolition as standing on Waterside and looking at numbers 30, 31 and Palmer's Court, the brickwork appears not to be as old as that on the cottages to the right. Marie's secretary, Annie Davis, lived at number 58, later basing her shorthand and typing school there, where the Rudolph Kempe Society is now.

In 1915 Marie was outraged when she heard about the potential lopping of the avenue of trees leading to Holy Trinity Church, instigated by the then vicar, William Melville, although it turned out that the lopping of the trees was really 'topping' or 'crowning' so they didn't come down in winter winds.

In 1916 she urged the Guild to pay for the uncovering and preservation of the old timbers at 30 High Street. Estimated at £75 (over £7000 today) Marie contributed £60 (about £5.5k) and the Guild £15 (about £1.5k). The premises were owned by her old adversary, Fred Winter, but that didn't stop Marie from contributing, or Winter from accepting.

At the beginning of 1920 plans for the restoration of the gardens at New Place (Shakespeare's last home) were in full swing, with a number of donors, including Queen Alexandra and the Earl of Pembroke, gifting plants. According to Roy Strong in his *The Quest for Shakespeare's Garden*, Marie 'had saved the day by contributing a cheque for £50 towards the planting of Ernest Law's New Place garden.'

Still, life for Marie and Bertha wasn't all fights with the town council, and conservation projects. There were also some fun times to be had.

Tudor House with Stucco, 1902-03
(Holte Collection, SBT)

CHAPTER 7
FESTIVITIES

The coronation of George V in 1911, was a good excuse for a Shakespeare Ball, held in the Albert Hall. In her unpublished manuscript, *The Magnificent Marie*, Enid Stuart Scott writes that:

> Marie attended in the guise of... her hero's sadly-neglected wife Anne Hathaway. She wore the 'Sunday best' costume of a Warwickshire peasant lass of Tudor times

the final authentic touch of which was a corsage of rosemary from Anne Hathaway's Shottery cottage.

Moving on a few years, during the First World War practically every fete and festival run by non-combatants raised money for the Allies, local hospitals and the Red Cross.

Jann Tracy

For Russia Day, Thursday 10 August 1916, Ludford Docker (first-class cricketer and President of Warwickshire CCC, later High Sheriff of Warwickshire) and his wife, held a charitable fete, in aid of the British Red Cross, at their house, Alveston Leys, in Stratford, for which they had excellent weather. Marie and Bertha had put down a deposit on the house when they were looking for a permanent home in the town, but then Marie decided that it was too near the river and would probably be damp.

The fete was part of the Summer Festival of Shakespeare's Tercentenary year which had brought American actress Mary Anderson out of retirement to play Hermione in *The Winter's Tale* (she was the first actress to play both Hermione and Perdita). Among the attractions was a sixpenny stall, run by Marie, Bertha and Mary Anderson, and on this stall were 100 boxes of chocolates, donated by Tommy Lipton; the stall was unsurprisingly, very popular. The photograph shows Marie with a young admirer in the grounds of Alveston Leys.

Marie was always in demand as a speaker at various events, due to her fame, willingness to attend, and amiability when giving prizes. But, as well as attending fetes and fairs, Marie continued to write, her focus now on the war effort. The following chapter details some of the publications she was involved with.

Alveston Leys Fete
Marie Corelli and young friend, c1916

CHAPTER 8
WARTIME

Before the declaration of the First Word War, Marie was inclined to be a pacifist, and wrote against fighting, not believing that war was a way to solve problems. Her novella, *Boy*, published in June 1900, has its hero killed in a Boer War battle. A surgeon at the Front tells a nurse:

> you must remember that the arts and sciences are very seldom rewarded - whereas if you kill a few of your human brethren you get notice and promotion.

At the outbreak of hostilities in 1914, however, she became fiercely patriotic, though still against the concepts of war, fighting and killing. To that end, she produced a number of small publications, in which she shared her personal views.

The World in Tears, November 1915

This small book encapsulated the feelings of those 'at home' during the First World War. It aimed to ameliorate the suffering of those who'd lost their loved ones on the battlefield, with proceeds going to the British Red Cross Society.

It contains pieces from not just Marie but other well-known writers such as Jerome K Jerome, as well as adherents to both the Protestant and Catholic faiths, those who follow the Jewish way, Spiritualism and the teachings of Buddha, and those who follow no faith at all. A unique coming together at a time of national conflict.

In 1915 the war that was supposed to have ended by Christmas 1914 was still killing and maiming thousands on and off the battlefields. Those at home were weary and dispirited and tired of exhortations to send their sons and husbands to the trenches. There seemed no possible end to the conflict and then a mother's letter was printed in a national newspaper, detailing her anguish at the loss of her son. *The World in Tears* was published in response.

The Rev J Stratton wrote in the book that the 'best source of comfort for fathers and mothers whose sons are fighting the nation's battles, must surely be found in the conviction that the latter are risking their lives in a righteous cause.' He was in the minority. In her preface Marie refers to 'this unspeakably wicked war... this most un-Christian world-contest.' Poet and novelist John Oxenham said of the young men who marched off so proudly, 'they have gone, most of them, from a simple, high sense of duty, and in many cases under direst feelings of personal repulsion against the whole ghastly business.'

The titles of the pieces belie the general anti-war feeling of the book: 'Life grows through noble sacrifice'; 'One day tears will be wiped away'; 'Their life is not closed, but only transfigured and glorified'. One contributor quoted from Shakespeare and one from the Bhagavad Gita (Hindu scripture in Sanskrit). Several called the nation's leaders to account, like Marie: 'for war and the murder of the many is always the result of the evil thoughts and passions of a misguided few.' Writer and political activist Israel Zangwill wrote: 'this tragic butchery... would be to deprive death of its reality... and war-makers of their guilt.'

Whether it proved successful in its aim of providing succour for those suffering is not known, nothing like it has been published since, perhaps because the hope of Sir WH Lever has not been fulfilled: 'It is the duty of the living to do all that one generation can do to make the recurrence of such barbarisms impossible in the future.'

Shakespeare at School, May 1916

In the Archives Collections of the SBT is a printed booklet entitled *Shakespeare at School*. This was a speech given by Marie to the boys of the Stratford-on-Avon Grammar School, on 2 May 1916, commemorating the tercentenary of Shakespeare's death. The school is now known as King Edward VI school, or KES.

Marie started her speech by telling the boys that the subject she was to talk about was one that for 300 years 'has interested the whole intellectual world.' She talks of Warwickshire being noted in 1549 by Becon (writer of *The Jewel of Joy*) as, 'the most intellectual of English counties,' and says if this was so then, 'what must it, what ought it to be now, three hundred years after [Shakespeare's] death... the mind almost staggers at the thought of such a store of ripened wit and wisdom!'

It is both an amusing portrait of Shakespeare as a boy, and rousingly patriotic, after all, there was a war on, and some of those boys in the audience might, in a few months, be heading to the Front to fight in the trenches of the Somme.

In his School's Speech Day address (26 July 1916) the then headmaster, Rev. A Cecil Knight, reported on her talk, and described it as wholly appropriate and entirely delightful and inspiring, and noted that, 'Miss Corelli has since presented a beautiful copy of her address to every member of the school.' He also informed the boys that she had offered a gold medal, to be presented annually, for the best two essays that show knowledge of Shakespeare in the broadest sense, to be judged by Sir Sidney Lee, Chairman of the SBT.

We see again, that Marie was at her best and most loved when she was playing the role of champion and Lady Bountiful.

A Happy Thoughts Day and a Happy Occasion, July 1916

The booklet entitled *A "happy thoughts" Day* was written to try and bring a more positive note to the dark days of war, and was sold at a fete held on Saturday 16 July 1916, to raise money for the Grantham Red Cross Outings Fund - every shilling meant one wounded soldier at the local Red Cross Hospital could go on an outing. This little booklet even found its way to South Australia, where at the end of the war, the *Adelaide Advertiser* of 14 November 1918 used its title in an advertisement for the film version of Marie's novel, *The Sorrows of Satan*, starring Gladys Cooper.

With Shakespeare in his Garden, July-August 1916

In an effort to attract tourists in the middle of the war, Marie wrote a pamphlet entitled *With*

Marie Corelli: Shakespeare's Champion

Shakespeare in his Garden. An Invitation to the Summer Festival at Stratford-upon-Avon from July 29 to August 26 1916, to accompany the packed programme of events. Waxing lyrical about the beauties of 'leafy Warwickshire, the most beautiful County in England' her words capture the general mood after two years of war, and the longing to escape from constant worry and strain. She enticed visitors with the promise of multiple and varied entertainments, such as the children of the Guild of Play who were to present Old English Dances, and Dances of the Allies. There were to be performances of *The Comedy of Errors* and *Two Gentlemen of Verona* which could be seen in the theatre, along with two Sheridan plays (it was his centenary). Audiences could hear music from Shakespeare's time, played on the instruments of that time by skilful musicians. The event was also notable for the participation of Miss Lilian Baylis, who would bring her new Shakespeare Repertory Company from London, among whom was the young Sybil Thorndyke. Lilian Baylis was at the time in charge of the Old Vic.

My Little Bit, published in 1919, is a collection of 50 articles written by Marie between 1914 and 1918. Many of the articles take to task the efforts of various bureaucrats to enforce rationing and other restrictions.

Her war efforts weren't only by her pen and sustaining morale. She offered Mason Croft as a hospital, but unfortunately the rooms were deemed to be too small and Clopton House was chosen instead.

After America entered the war, in April 1917, she offered Trinity College, free of rent, as a convalescent home for wounded American soldiers, paying all expenses, and with free use of the paddock. It was opened by the American General Biddle in December 1918, to receive, not fighting soldiers, but sight-seeing soldiers returning home after the Armistice. The townsfolk saw this as a contribution to the economic upturn of their fortunes. Sixteen years after the Henley Street furore Marie was still making a difference in the town, and for once, being recognised and appreciated for it. Unfortunately, due to lack of funds the convalescent home closed in April 1919. After

Marie's death in 1924 the college building was sold.

The Sketch

No. 672.—Vol. LII. WEDNESDAY, DECEMBER 13, 1905. SIXPENCE.

A PHOTOGRAPH OF A LADY WHO WILL NOT BE PHOTOGRAPHED. A SNAPSHOT OF MISS MARIE CORELLI LEAVING HER CAB AT THE PORTLAND ROOMS TO ATTEND THE SHAKSPEAREAN BAZAAR.

Caption: A photograph of a lady who will not be photographed. A snapshot of Miss Marie Corelli leaving her cab at the Portland Rooms to attend the Shakespearean Bazaar.

CHAPTER 9
REPUTATION

Marie and Bertha had arrived in Stratford hoping to settle happily and be accepted, but her strong opinions and determination to save old buildings were not always appreciated or understood fully at the time, and her reputation suffered great highs and lows during her lifetime. Marie was a conservationist long before the name and its aims were familiar everyday terms, and there were those in the town who didn't like it when the sociable woman and Lady Bountiful turned Lady Conservationist.

Although they tried to ignore her, the council resented the way in which she spent her money, even though it was for good causes. Stratford-upon-Avon had for many years been run by the men who ran the shops, newspapers and opinion in the town, such as FC Westwood, Birthplace secretary, Salt Brassington, theatre librarian, Fred Winter, draper, George Lea, butcher, Kibler Morgan, estate agent, JH Rowe, farmer and owner of the racecourse, George Boyden, newspaper editor, all, incidentally, members of the Freemasons' Swan of Avon Lodge. It was a fearsome group to go against.

Marie always had detractors as she was unmarried and successfully earning her own living.

Asked on one occasion why she did not marry, Marie is said to have replied:

> I have three pets at home which together answer the same purpose as a husband. I have a dog which growls all the morning, a parrot which swears all the afternoon and a cat which comes home late at night.

The reality was that she was fiercely independent, and also, might not have found the right person. The issue of her relationships has always been a grey area.

Marie Corelli: Shakespeare's Champion

The Rev. Harvey Bloom, an early friend and supporter, was acting master of Trinity College, next door to Mason Croft, and introduced his seven-year old daughter Ursula to Marie. Ursula Bloom went on to write over 500 novels.

In 1902, however, Bloom and Marie fell out because he and his wife had apparently discussed, in front of Ursula, the possibility of Marie being divorced and, ever protective of her reputation, she severed contact between the two households. She later caricatured him in a 1904 novel, *God's Good Man*, showing that Marie could sometimes be unforgiving.

Not trusting the objectivity of the local paper, Marie published *The Avon Star. A Literary Manual for the Stratford-upon-Avon Season of 1903*, containing Shakespeare-related articles by various writers, plus her views on the town, the Faucit Memorial, and, of course, Henley Street.

Harvey Bloom retaliated with *Errors of the Avon Star*, which was an unpleasant and personal attack on Marie.

Unfortunately, it was now apparent that there were pro- and anti-Marie factions in the town. The bitterness escalated, culminating in her bringing an action for libel against the *Stratford-upon-Avon Herald*, and a certain Fred Winter. This is because, in June 1903, Fred Winter wrote a letter to the *Herald* in which he stated that Marie had asked him to enquire about the price of the land next to the Technical School 'for the purposes of a Free Library.' Marie decided the price was too high and the land was subsequently bought by Archie Flower. Winter suggests that Marie wasn't against a library in Henley Street, just that she wanted it to be a 'Corelli' rather than a 'Carnegie' library. The *Herald* published Winter's letter along with an unflattering editorial on Marie, and on the same day Fred Winter sent both his letter and the *Herald*'s editorial to all the major national newspapers with a covering letter asking that both be published.

The anti-Marie faction also published their point of view in a pamphlet in the summer of 1903, but, interestingly, had trouble placing it as establishments such as the Army and Navy stores and Hatchards refused to sell it.

At the subsequent libel trial, the jury found for the plaintiff, Marie, but awarded her one farthing in damages. The judge observed that obviously the matter should not have been brought to trial.

The farthing was eventually paid by Fred Winter, and subsequently returned by Marie, 'as a contribution to one of the many Stratford charities he no doubt supports.' Winter established a Farthing Fund for the benefit of a Stratford hospital; Marie sent him 12,000 farthings (around £12 10s at the time, over £1,300 now), which he returned. Neither Marie nor Winter was willing to back down.

She could be insensitive to the feelings of others and was unable to understand why her 'dear scribe' Annie Davis felt compelled to leave her employ after Marie gave the sole care of her gondola to Ernest Chandler, one-time gardener, now full-time gondolier. The gondola had until then been cared for by Annie's father and brother who ran a boat business from their Waterside cottage. The gondola was too big to be moored with Marie's other boats opposite Waterside and was kept in some old arches near to the church. Marie thought she was doing both parties a favour by giving Ernest sole responsibility for the gondola, but Annie's father was deeply hurt and refused to have any more to do with *any* of Marie's boats. Torn between loyalty and affection for her employer, and love for her family, Annie handed in her notice. Many years later Annie was asked to give a talk about her erstwhile employer and said she would only talk of the happy times. Although deeply upset by Marie's behaviour, Annie remained loyal to the end.

Marie's reputation was severely dented during the First World War when she was accused of food hoarding. In 1917 Mason Croft orchards and gardens had produced about 1,000 lbs worth of apples and plums. Regulations in force at the time stated that sugar for jam making must be supplied locally through use of the ration card. The local shops weren't able to supply her with the quantities needed to turn all her fruit into jam, so she contacted her old friend Tommy Lipton who arranged for crates of sugar to be delivered to Mason Croft. Local tradesmen were angry that she had gone elsewhere for supplies, despite their inability to provide enough sugar, and contacted the authorities. A policeman searched the house but could find no hidden bags of sugar. Regardless of the lack of evidence, the matter went to court.

The magistrates bench consisted of Fred Winter, George Boyden and other of her local foes. Marie didn't attend court; Bertha was questioned but her evidence discounted; all the Mason Croft servants were in court, but not called on to give evidence. Marie was found guilty of food hoarding, fined £50 (nearly £5,500 today) and ordered to pay costs of 50 guineas (over £5,700 now). Though convicted on a technicality, the press had a field day with their banner headlines. She received letters accusing her of hypocrisy, but many more from her supporters, appalled at the pettiness of the conviction.

In her book, *Memoirs of Marie Corelli*, published in 1930, Bertha recalls these events:

> As I said, to-day the whole thing is comedy, but at the time Marie's treatment by citizens of a town on which she had spent thousands of pounds on its restoration alone, thus largely increasing its beauty and historic interest, and therefore,

its trade, hurt her at the time deeply.

Marie's books are not much read now, but her reputation as a pioneer of 'things to come' deserves recognition. For example, she wrote of her first novel, *A Romance of Two Worlds*, (1886) that, 'it was an eager, though crude attempt... to write of radium, that wonderful 'discovery' of the immediate hour.'

She says that although she was only allowed to use the word electricity, that was not so far off the mark 'seeing that electric force displays itself in countless millions of forms.' Her theory of the universe in the novel preceded a 1905 piece in the *Hibbert Journal* by a scientist who concluded his article, 'Electricity is all things, and all things are electric.' Although this was what she herself had written, she says she was ridiculed for it:

> I was told that there was no spiritual force in electricity. I differ from this view, but radio-activity is perhaps the better... as scientists have proved - Radium is capable of

> absorbing from surrounding bodies some unknown form of energy which it can render evident as heat and light.

The Reverend William Stuart Scott, an admirer of Marie's novels, claimed that *The Life Everlasting* (1911) prophesied, 'the hydrogen bomb, and the application of atomic power to transport... She seems to have had faith in scientific progress: sound waves, light rays, microbes, electricity, radium - all are treated in her novels, not only after the war but from the very beginning of her career.'

J Cuming Walters, in an epilogue in Bertha's Memoir wrote, 'In the realm of speculative science Miss Corelli... preceded Wells.'

The invention in 1910 of a method of communication between moving trains and stations or signal boxes, caught the public imagination. Hans von Kramer, a Birmingham electrical engineer, one day noticed that an amount of electric power was passing through a brick wall, from one coil of electric wire to another coil. He later found that he could pass sound waves through walls six feet thick and subsequently invented the Railophone. Messages could be sent and delivered while a train was moving at 40 miles an hour. This is the sort of invention that attracted Marie and her interest in the modernity of things, which was demonstrated by her at the old Stratford railway station. In April 1911, she performed the inaugural ceremony, talking from a signal box to a train driver.

It was later reported in the *Marlborough Express*, a New Zealand paper, in May 1911:

> The system is being now installed, in a more perfected form, on the Stratford-on-Avon and Midland Junction railway. Visitors travelling on the line to the Shakspere [sic] festival will find the "railophone" in working order, and be able to test some of its wonderful qualities.
> [National Library of New Zealand - Papers Past]

1921 saw the publication of *The Secret Power* predicting germ warfare and the atom bomb; communication through sound waves which transmit voice without wires [radio]; light rays which beam pictures through vast distances [television]; force fields, and the use of the sun's energy for power [solar panels]. All of these ideas became common knowledge in the twentieth-century.

In *The Secret Power* one of her characters explains:

> You know the use of wireless telephony... We speak as Sound Rays... We need neither transmitter nor receiver. Wherever we send our messages, no matter how great the distance, they are always heard.
>
> [Our city is] surrounded by a belt of etheric force through which nothing can pass. A million bombs could not break it. [In our time various US administrations have been trying to create much the same sort of thing].

Although prone to extreme views and great stubbornness, Marie was also able to change her mind, if circumstances allowed. She used to call suffragettes 'ladies who scream', but, like so many others, her attitudes on various topics were changed by the experiences of the First World War.

In a tract written by her, *Is All Well with England?* published by Jarrolds, London, 1919, she states quite frankly that she had previously been strongly opposed to the Votes for Women campaign as she thought it unnecessary. But during the war women had taken over many of the jobs previously held by men who were now on the battlefields and in the trenches, and so had proved themselves as capable as the male of the species, at all sorts of hard graft. She ends the piece in favour of the suffragists:

> it *was* and *is* no longer possible to deny them equal rights with men in every relation of life and every phase of work. By every law of justice they should have the vote – and I who, as a woman, was once against it, now most ardently support the cause.

Marie Corelli: Shakespeare's Champion

Even after her death in 1924 Marie's reputation still divided opinion - but quite a few of the papers wrote about her in admiring editorials.

The Daily Telegraph:

> [She] wielded a most vigorous pen... never afraid to utter her opinions with extreme... sometimes disconcerting frankness... was endowed with an imagination of unbounded scope... aimed directly at the heart of the people... Whatever was in her mind came forth with all the turbulence of a river in spate. And the public adored her.

The Evening Standard:

> Her charity was great and frequently, if quietly, expressed. In the passing of Miss Marie Corelli a great figure in the fiction of the last 30 years is lost, to the regret of

many friends and a world wide public.

The Manchester Guardian:

> She was famous in her twenties, and earned as much money in a few years as many of the modern masters of literature made in a lifetime... one cannot help thinking now that she was born before her time.

Tennis at Mason Croft, c1922

Marie Corelli: Shakespeare's Champion

CHAPTER 10
DEATH AND AFTERWARDS

Marie had a heart attack in January 1924, and died on 21 April, which was Easter Monday that year, and two days before the annual Shakespeare Birthday celebrations. Her long-term antagonist, the *Stratford-upon-Avon Herald* wrote: 'That Miss Corelli succeeded in making the town a prettier place than she entered must be generously admitted.' Her funeral was attended by townsfolk and dignitaries, both friend and foe.

Despite rain on the day, there was a large crowd following the funeral procession, with a band playing. At Mason Croft the band passed by in silence. The church was packed, with people gathering outside.

Sadly, Marie is now largely forgotten and ignored in the town. There is only the board in the Firs Gardens, and a couple of plaques on the wall of Mason Croft. There was a school named after her, but sadly this closed in 2000. There is also a Corelli Close in Bishopton, and interestingly a Corelli Road in Basingstoke.

Marie and Bertha are side by side in the town cemetery, on Evesham Road. Her tomb with its accompanying angel, shipped by Bertha from Italy in 1924, was vandalised in December 2012 (along with a number of other graves) and the angel removed to storage. On 5 July 2017 the angel was restored to its place of honour, thanks to the Town Council, author Teresa Ransom and the Stratford Society.

Despite divided opinions about her, her death brought recognition of her influence in opposing modernisation in Stratford, in the form of a tribute printed in *The Times*, written by Sir Sidney Lee, Life Trustee of the SBT. After describing her as an outstanding personality with an independent mind and combative spirit, he acknowledges her beneficial role in the town:

> By her influence or at her own cost many of the houses in the town were preserved when they were

threatened with rebuilding on modern lines... her intervention [had the effect of] modifying at a crucial point the original plan of demolition [on Henley Street] in a manner which has proved of real benefit [to the SBT].

Marie Corelli's Funeral Cortege, 1924

CONCLUSION

Despite Roy Strong's scathing description of her as a 'short, fat... female of repellent aspect' even he has to concede that she 'bestowed a large part of her wealth to ensure that what was left of the playwright's town was not swept away.'

Marie was always greatly concerned about her appearance, and allowed only photographs approved by herself to be distributed. The SBT archives hold several 'before and after' photos, evidence of alteration by the photographer. Candid shots of Marie show a small woman with quite a sweet face. I think she did herself no favours with her obsession over her looks, and would hate the proliferation of cameras today. On the other hand, I think she would take to today's air-brushed 'celebrity-type' photograph. Also, I'm sure she would be a keen blogger and tweeter, and have a strong Facebook presence - she wouldn't be able to resist such a potentially large audience!

As part of the Shakespearean Quatercentenary Celebrations a Corelli Exhibition (9 June to 3 July 1964) was held at Mason Croft and opened by the then mayor. There were rumours of her ghost haunting the exhibition.

Her books were written with the superfluity of words beloved by Victorians, but her ideas were in advance of their time, with their use of electricity and aeroplanes and references to force fields and atom bombs. In her books she attempted to reconcile her Christian beliefs with scientific discoveries, as well as reincarnation, astral projection and other ideas which today are regarded as the basis of New Age beliefs.

Despite being opposed by the local cabal of councillors and freemasons that ran the town, she managed to keep the locals and tourists on her side, and her staff remained fiercely loyal during her life and after her death.

Walk around Stratford-upon-Avon today and look at the wonderful old buildings that still exist. Give thanks to Marie Corelli for her championship of Shakespeare's home town. It wouldn't look the same without her.

Marie Corelli in her Conservatory at Mason Croft

APPENDICES

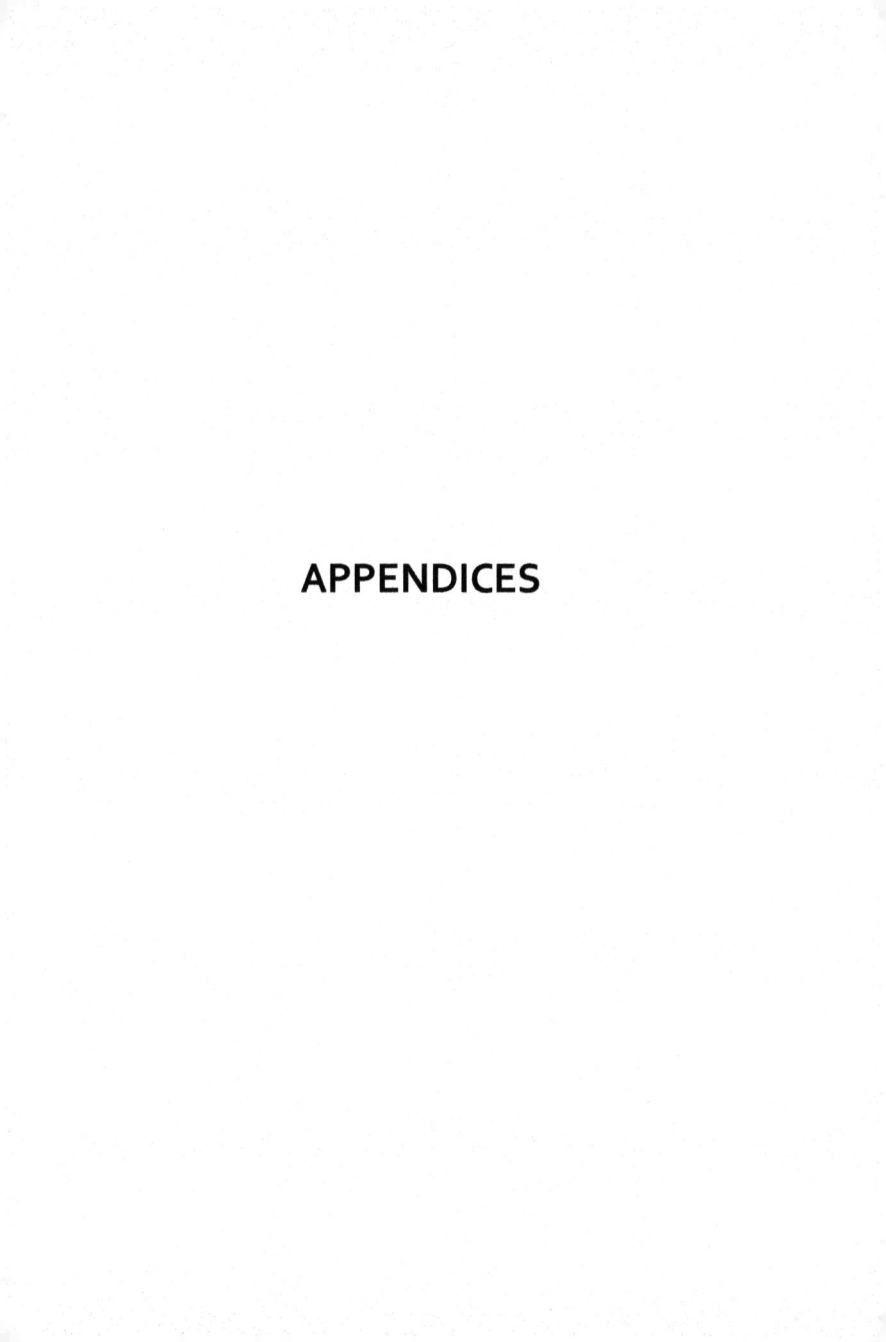

APPENDIX A: Early Life
The years before Stratford

Marie Corelli spent her adult life obscuring her origins, and the facts of her birth. In the Victorian age, illegitimacy was guaranteed to keep anyone outside of the mainstream. Marie Corelli started life as Mary Mills, the illegitimate daughter of Elizabeth Mary (Ellen) Mills and Charles Mackay. Mackay was a journalist already married with four children when he began his liaison with Ellen Mills.

Due to this affair his wife left him in 1853, and two years later young Mary was born. Mary and her mother lived together in London until 1861 when Mackay and Mills married. By then he was a widower, his wife having died the previous year. Little Mary Mills then became Minnie Mackay, living with her parents at 18 Avenue Road, a large house, now demolished, near Regent's Park in London.

Mackay formally adopted his daughter, which was a well-used way in Victorian times of legitimising children born outside wedlock. Having now to support another family Mackay began to have financial problems and was granted a literary pension by Lord Palmerston of £100 a year.

In February 1862 the family moved to America, living in New York where Minnie's father worked as a reporter on *The Times* newspaper, covering the American civil war. In December 1863 the family returned to England for three months, living once again at 18 Avenue Road. Mackay returned to America alone, until finally returning to England in December 1865, having managed to alienate the American North in the war with his views on the South's right to secede if they wanted.

From 1866 to 1870 young Minnie was educated at a convent in Paris, holidaying in the summers with her father in Scotland. It was during this time that Minnie met the Countess van der Vyver and her daughter Bertha and the two girls became lifelong friends.

By 1871 the Mackays were all living at Fern Dell Cottage, Box Hill and according to the census return the household consisted of Mackay 56, Ellen 41, Minnie 16, a cook and a maid. Mackay was a freelance journalist who also wrote poems and novels. By all accounts the young Minnie, like the young Virginia Woolf, was allowed free run of her father's library, but had no companions of her own age.

Ellen became very ill and by 1875, at the suggestion of the Countess, Bertha Vyver joined the Mackay household. Ellen died in February 1876 and Minnie and Bertha took over the running of the household. That same year education became compulsory and so a new generation could become readers of newspapers, novels and penny dreadfuls (cheap, highly popular and sensational serial literature, often garishly illustrated).

Minnie's first attempt at a novel, written in indelible pencil in an exercise book contains a conversation between the villain and the heroine:

> 'You are an admirer of Beethoven's music Miss Graham.'
>
> 'Of course. Are you?'
>
> 'No, fact is, I can't endure it. Beethoven occupies the same position in my mind as Shakespeare - both of them very much overrated

> men. They couldn't have stood a chance in our day.'

In the light of Marie's later professed and obvious admiration for Shakespeare, this could be seen as a small piece of irony.

According to the census return of 1881 living at Fern Dell are Mackay 67, Eric 46 (Mackay's middle son from his first marriage who gave his age as 40 to the census) Minnie 26 and Bertha 27 (they both gave their ages as 22). Eric Mackay was a failure in everything he tried, for example, taking money from his father for years while supposedly training in Italy as a singer, leading instead a dissolute life. He was to be a drain on Minnie/Marie's resources for the rest of his life.

In June 1883 Charles Mackay had a stroke and the family moved to 47 Longridge Road, Kensington, continuing to live in genteel poverty. Between 1882-83 Minnie worked at building a career as singer and pianist, giving several concerts, but her voice wasn't strong enough for her to be a professional, and she found it a great strain to play the piano in front of an audience. She was soon however to find her career and her new name, which she first used in May 1883 in a letter to the editor of *Blackwood's Magazine* asking that he publish some of her poems. She didn't sign the letter, but referred to herself as Signorina Marie Corelli.

July 1885 saw her first acceptance as an author with an article titled 'One of the World's Wonders', for which she was paid 10 guineas, over £500 today. It was published in *Temple Bar* and described a shell cave she'd visited in Margate.

Her first novel, *A Romance of Two Worlds*, was published on 19 February 1886, in two volumes, by George Bentley. It is a story of electrical communication, space and time travel, electric bell pushes and door openers, electric lighting, impenetrable force fields, travel to other worlds and *eternal youth*.

> At one time people mocked at the wild idea that a message could flash from one side of the Atlantic to the other by means of a cable laid under the sea; [the Atlantic Cable was laid finally in 1865]... why should not a

> communication be established...
> between man and beings of other...
> solar systems?

Scientists have tried in the past to send radio messages into space, and NASA's Pioneer 10 (launched in 1972) and Pioneer 11 (launched in 1973) spacecraft both carried messages written on plaques and a record. In 1997 Voyager I, which recently left our solar system, carried a golden record containing images and words about life on earth. In 2014 NASA called for messages from 'ordinary people' to be beamed up to space probe New Horizons ready for when it leaves its present orbit of Pluto and goes inter-stellar. And so life imitates Art.

Rider Haggard's *She* (set in Africa with a white queen, Ayesha, who has been granted the secret of *eternal youth*) was published the year after *A Romance of Two Worlds*. Marie published this novel containing time travel nine years before HG Wells published his best-selling book *The Time Machine*. Though he is credited with popularising the concept of time travel, Marie put it into print first.

Marie Corelli: Shakespeare's Champion

In July 1886 *Vendetta* was published. The world was changing, with scientists challenging clergy with their ideas about the natural world. The bicycle, as opposed to the penny farthing, could now be ridden by brave women, who could escape from the confines of Victorian drawing rooms. Marie was tapping into the zeitgeist with her own brand of the perfect escapist novel, mixing mysticism, spiritualism, science and romance.

August 1886 and Marie was on holiday on her own in Scotland, rowing and fishing. This was possibly when she met the love of her life. I cannot find much on this subject, but it is hinted at in various books about her.

Thelma was published in June 1887. Marie invented the name, which made it into the top 100 names in the UK in 1924 and 1934, and into the top 100 names in the US between 1900 and 1910. She wrote to Bertha about *Thelma*, 'that is to be your book, and the world will know that Bertha is Marie Corelli's dearest friend.'

Ardath was published in 1889, sealing Marie's fame and she became a celebrity in London, meeting many famous people. Her stepfather died in December 1889, after a protracted illness, and was buried in January 1890. He left his entire estate to Minnie and appointed her his executrix; Eric was left nothing. In April they nursed Bertha's mother, the Countess van der Vyver until her death. In quick succession Marie had lost her father, whom she adored, and the woman who had been a mother figure for much of her life. A month later, in May, needing a break from the grief felt in London, Marie, Bertha and Eric stayed at the Falcon Hotel in Stratford-upon-Avon for ten days.

Wormwood, describing the horrors of absinthe drinkers in Paris, a city of which Marie had a poor opinion, was published in November 1890, and the first edition sold out in ten days.

1892 saw the publication of *The Soul of Lilith*, another outstanding success with the public, if not the critics. In this year she went to stay in Homburg and was feted by royalty in the person of the Prince of Wales (later King Edward VII). She was invited to dine with him and reported to Bertha that he knew all her books and talked about different scenes in them. At a later lunch, the Prince introduced her to his second son, Prince George (later King George V) who also enjoyed her books. She had definitely 'arrived'.

Perhaps it was around this time that a rose was named in her honour. A fragrant, salmon pink hybrid perpetual. Hybrid perpetuals are the link between the old rose and the modern hybrid tea. They were not only the most popular roses for garden and indoors during the Victorian era, they remained popular for over 60 years. Probably due to their limited colour range of white, pink and red, and a lack of reliable reflowering, they were finally overtaken by the ever popular hybrid teas. But, in their heyday, they were absolutely *the* roses to grow!

Upon her return from Homburg Marie became embroiled in the affair of *The Silver Domino*, written partly by Marie, her brother Eric and a close friend called Henry Labouchere. The book is an attack upon and lampoon of Maire's contemporaries in politics and literature and she was ostracised by many as a result, although it's probable that Eric and Henry changed the text she had seen before her trip, making it darker and more spiteful. George Bentley, who had supported her and published all her novels so far was particularly incensed by *The Silver Domino*'s depiction of publishers. When he retired his son Richard took over the business, and there was mutual antipathy between him and Marie. So one of the far-reaching results of this satirical publication was her change in publisher from Bentley to Methuen.

Her first book with Methuen was *Barabbas*, written from the point of view of the thief who was pardoned. It was published in October 1893 and subsequently in over 40 languages. Parts of it were often read out in church, especially on the day of resurrection at Easter.

1895 saw a revolution in the way books were distributed as they became available straight to the public, from public libraries and booksellers, rather than only through the circulating libraries. While some more literary authors missed out as a result, those who were popular with the public benefited. Marie published *The Sorrows of Satan* under the new system, and, reluctant to allow the critics to snipe at another of her novels, decided that no free review copies were to be sent out. As Teresa Ransom says, 'The initial sales of *The Sorrows of Satan* in 1895 were greater than any previous novel written in English.' Father Ignatius, a monk from Abergavenny, gave two sermons at the

Portman Rooms, Baker Street, London, where he said: 'Marie Corelli is doing more for the faith than Archbishops and Bishops and convocations put together... Let all our clergy have a copy of *The Sorrows of Satan* on their literary tables.'

In March 1896 *The Mighty Atom* was produced by Hutchinson's in return for them publishing a book of Eric's poems. The poems were not a success, Marie's book was.

Life was not all plain sailing, however and in December 1897 Marie went to Hove to have what was probably an hysterectomy, undertaken by a friend of her and Bertha, Dr Mary Scharlieb. Marie and Bertha then moved to the King's Private Hotel in Brighton for the three months of Marie's convalescence.

In April 1898 she and Bertha moved to a suite at the Royal Hotel, Woodhall Spa in Lincolnshire where they planned to stay for a long while, Marie having grown tired of the racket of London. However, in June 1898 Eric died of heart failure following pneumonia and Marie and Bertha returned to London.

A few months later in September, after a stay in Scotland following her collapse from stress, Marie discovered that Eric had been systematically cheating her and blackening her name to all and sundry. She decided to move from London and Dr Scharlieb recommended that Marie spent at least two years elsewhere.

Remembering the happy time they'd had in Stratford-upon-Avon eight years earlier, that became their destination of choice.

APPENDIX B: Timeline

May 1855 Mary Mills is born in London to Charles Mackay and Elizabeth Mary (Ellen) Mills. Mary and Ellen live in London

[Another version of this story is that the baby was the result of a liaison between Mackay's daughter Rosa and operatic tenor Signor Corelli. Rosa died in Italy (aged 17) the year Mary was born and thus she would have been Mackay's granddaughter]

February 1861 Mackay and Ellen Mills marry; thereafter the daughter is known as Minnie Mackay and the family live at 18 Avenue Road, Regent's Park

February 1862 The family move to America, living in New York

December 1863 The family return to England for three months, living at 18 Avenue Road

1866-70 Minnie is educated at a convent in Paris

1868-69 At some point in this period Minnie meets Countess van der Vyver and her daughter Bertha

1871 According to the census return the family living at Fern Dell Cottage, Box Hill comprises Charles Mackay 56, Ellen 41 and Minnie 16

1875 Ellen becomes very ill. Bertha Vyver joins the Mackay household

February 1876 Ellen dies

1881 The census return says that the household living at Fern Dell are Charles Mackay 67, Eric 46 (Mackay's middle son from his first marriage), Minnie 26 and Bertha 27

June 1883 Charles Mackay has a stroke and the family move to 47 Longridge Road, Kensington

1882-83 Minnie attempts a career as singer and pianist, giving several concerts

July 1885 Marie's first acceptance as an author is an article published in *Temple Bar*

19 February 1886 *A Romance of Two Worlds* is published in two volumes by George Bentley

July 1886 *Vendetta* is published

August 1886 Marie is on holiday in Scotland, rowing and fishing

June 1887 *Thelma* is published

1889 Marie becomes a celebrity in London, meeting many famous people

December 1889 Charles Mackay dies

January 1890 Marie uses the name Minnie Mackay for the last time in a letter to *Blackwood's Magazine* regarding the publication of her father's last poem

April 1890 Countess van der Vyver dies

May 1890 Marie, Bertha and Eric stay at the Falcon Hotel in Stratford-upon-Avon for ten days

Jann Tracy

November 1890 *Wormwood* is published. This is a tale of an addict and his journey to despair due to alcohol. The first edition sells out in 10 days

1892 *The Soul of Lilith* is published. A combination of romance and spiritualism, it is enormously popular

October 1893 *Barabbas* is published. By the end of the following year it's in its 14th edition and is one of her most popular novels

1895 Her most famous novel, *The Sorrows of Satan*, is published and becomes the best-selling book of the year

December 1897 Marie is in Hove to have an operation. Marie and Bertha move to Brighton for Marie's convalescence

April 1898 She and Bertha move direct from Brighton to the Royal Hotel, Woodhall Spa, Lincolnshire

June 1898 Eric dies. In September Marie discovers that he had been systematically cheating her and blackening her name to all and sundry for many years

1899 Marie and Bertha move to Stratford-upon-Avon, renting Hall's Croft from Mrs Croker. Later in the year they move to the Dower House

1900 Throughout the year Marie pays for outings for over 2000 schoolchildren

1900 Marie is elected President of Stratford-upon-Avon Choral Union and organises a sell-out concert. In July she organises a concert on the river with illuminated boats

October 1900 Marie offers to pay off Holy Trinity Church's debt. The Faucit memorial controversy

1901 Marie and Bertha move to Mason Croft

May 1901 Annie Davis starts work for Marie as her secretary

January 1902 Puck and Ariel and the pony trap are shipped from Scotland

1902 Marie and the Rev Harvey Bloom (next door neighbour at Trinity College) fall out

September 1902 The Bancroft Basin controversy

February 1903 Marie first writes to newspapers regarding the proposed Free Library in Henley Street

1903 Marie pays for the restoration of 23-24 High Street (Tudor House) giving £200 to AJ Stanley, the printer

1903 Marie publishes *The Avon Star*, soon followed by *Errors of the Avon Star* by Harvey Bloom

June 1903 Fred Winter writes a letter to the *Stratford-upon-Avon Herald* that results in Marie bringing a libel action against him and the paper

July 1903 A pamphlet, written by Sidney Lee, with the collaboration of several of Marie's opponents in the town, is rushed into print but no sellers want it on their shelves

December 1903 Marie wins one farthing in damages at the Birmingham Assizes for the libel case. Winter pays it, Marie returns it

September 1904 *God's Good Man* is published, caricaturing Harvey Bloom

By 1904 Marie is the author of 19 novels, two booklets and numerous articles. She is the single best-selling author, male or female, in Britain

Early 1905 sees her importing a Venetian gondola (*The Dream*) complete with gondolier

1905 Marie takes an interest in Harvard House

Summer 1905 Marie and Bertha are on board Tommy Lipton's yacht and meet Edward Morris and his wife

1908 Marie buys Trinity College

1909-10 The Firs house is sold and the gardens are bought by Marie. Harvard House is opened by the American Ambassador

1911 Railophone inauguration ceremony

1913 The Guild of Stratford, a conservation group, is formed with Marie on the committee

1914 Marie wants the Guild to protest against the felling of trees at Loxley and Welford, and works to Waterside cottages

1914 *Innocent* is published

1915 She has words with the vicar about the treatment of trees at Holy Trinity Church

1916 The Guild pays £15 towards uncovering and preserving old timbers at 30 High Street (Fred Winter's shop), Marie contributes £60

January 1918 Marie is summoned to the local magistrate's court to face a charge of sugar hoarding

1918 *The Young Diana* is published

1918 Trinity College is opened for American soldiers returning home after the war

1919 *Is All Well with England?* is published, in which she supports women's suffrage

1921 *The Secret Power* is published

1923 *Love and the Philosopher* is published

Christmas 1923 and she sends a chicken to each of the tenants of the almshouses

21 April 1924 Marie Corelli dies

Marie Corelli: Shakespeare's Champion

APPENDIX C : Changes to Henley St.
From Spennell's Enterprise Almanack and Annual with Directory

[if no occupation is specified, it's as previously]

	1901	1902	1903	1904
No.1	Mrs Lambert glass and china merchant	Mrs Lambert	Mrs Lambert	Mrs Lambert
Nos. 2 and 3	Henry Humphreys house furnisher	Henry Humphreys	Henry Humphreys	Henry Humphreys
No.4	Thomas Neale tin plate worker	Thomas Neale	Thomas Neale	Thomas Neale
No.5	William James Bryant fancy repository	William James Bryant	William James Bryant	William James Bryant
No.6	David Drinkwater boot warehouse	David Drinkwater	David Drinkwater	David Drinkwater
No.7	Giles Collins basket maker	Giles Collins	Giles Collins	Giles Collins
No.8	Not mentioned	Not mentioned	Bullard & Co (workshop)	Birch Bros
No.9	Mr & Mrs Albert Simms apartments	Mrs Albert Simms	Mr & Mrs Albert Simms	Mr & Mrs Albert Simms
No.10	John Henry Maries organ, etc, repairer	Mrs Howard, fruiterer	Mrs Howard	Mrs Howard
No.11	Technical School	Technical School	Technical School	Free public library
There had been a house next to the Technical School, which had burnt down a few years earlier, this space was incorporated into the library					
No.12	Birch Bros china, glass, etc, merchants	Birch Bros	Birch Bros	Free public library
After the demolition of the two cottages next to Birch's (Nos. 13 & 14) Nos. 15 & 16 (Hornby Cottages) were made into one building and re-numbered					
No.13	Abel Becket chimneysweep	Abel Becket	Abel Becket	Birthplace ticket office
No.14	Misses Birch	Mrs Birch	Mrs Birch	No longer exists
No.15	Joseph Savage butcher	Joseph Savage	Joseph Savage	No longer exists
No.16	George Yardley shoemaker	George Yardley	George Yardley and EC Unitt, bricklayer	No longer exists
Shakespeare's Birthplace					

APPENDIX D: Hall's Croft

Hall's Croft, formerly Cambridge House, once home to William Shakespeare's daughter Susanna and her husband Dr John Hall, had been owned by Mrs Catherine Croker since 1892, when she bought the freehold property for £2,500 (£212,526 approx. today). She had sometimes let it (as in 1899 to Marie Corelli), but in June 1913, the house came on the market. It was bought by American Josephine Macleod who moved in with her widowed sister Betty Leggett.

Betty oversaw the restoration of the house, taking it back to its Tudor appearance, stripping away the Victorianisms, stucco and faux gothic. Betty's daughter, Frances, describes in her book *Late and Soon*, how Betty filled the house with a plethora of objects:

> Never was there such a hotchpotch of English, Oriental, European of all ages; never did a house so express its owner... Betty always left the front door open so that people could see inside. Here was a house

of Shakespeare's day being actually lived in. This was unique in Stratford.

In those days the railway terminated at the East and West Junction railway station, near where the Greenway car park roundabout and Old Town Mews are now. When trains arrived at the station the streets were filled with people and sound as they walked to town via Old Town, being greeted by the sight of Hall's Croft, welcoming their arrival.

For that brief time prior to the First World War, Betty Leggett loved the old house, and the town, but was always travelling away from it, something she did for the rest of her life. In 1914-15 she was in the United States, but came back at various times, particularly on 26 April 1916 when Frances married David Margesson, (Viscount Margesson, who was Churchill's Secretary of State for War in the Second World War). There is a photograph in the SBT archives, of Frances in her wedding gown in the gardens of Hall's Croft.

Betty Leggett eventually returned to Hall's Croft and died there in 1931 after a fall down the stairs. The house remained in the family's hands until 1949 when it was bought by the SBT.

Betty's ghost is said to haunt the house, with visitors reporting feeling hands on their back as they stand at the top of the stairs.

APPENDIX E: Love and Marie Corelli

The pairing of romance and St Valentine was probably invented by Chaucer in the 14th century, and the earliest known 'valentines' were sent in the 15th century. St Valentine's Day even got a mention in *Hamlet*. It became big business in the 19th century; for example, in 1835, 60,000 valentine cards were sent by post in Britain and the custom still flourishes today. In an updated version, an estimated 15 million e-valentines were sent in 2010.

Although Marie Corelli was known as a romantic novelist, she wasn't a 'Mills & Boon' type of writer in the 19th century tradition, where the only options available for heroines were marriage or death. In many of Marie's novels and short stories, her independent heroines scorn the romantic. In the story 'The Soul of the Newly Born', midwife Nurse Collins declares:

> What *I* call real love is very different to what your fine gentleman of fashion calls it. To love a woman well enough to save her from any

> suspicion of slander is real love if you like.

Marie had an ideal of love between equals, where passion and the spiritual merged. Her eponymous heroine Diana (*The Young Diana*, 1918) declares, 'Love is the necessity of life to a woman', but her friend Sophy replies, 'Out of a thousand men taken at random perhaps one will really *love*, in the best and finest sense... your notion of 'love' is a dream, beyond all realisation!' Diana herself, after many adventures, concurs and declares at the end of her story, 'There is no such thing as love in all mankind.'

Marie famously remained unmarried, and declared that love, and only love justified marriage. I have previously mentioned a love interest in her early life, for which there is little evidence and the received wisdom is that she fell unhappily in love when in her fifties, with painter Arthur Severn, but he was a married man and had no intention of leaving his wife of more than forty years. She scorned her heroines who married for the sake of mere companionship or financial security, and upheld her unmarried artists who remained single rather than wed for such reasons. In a short story called 'Claudia's Business', the author remarks about one of her male protagonists:

> He laboured under the pleasing delusion, so common to the male sex, that any woman, no matter how independent, wealthy or beautiful, must, must, MUST be delighted with an offer of marriage, even if the wooer were but an uglier type of the simian ancestor according to Darwin.

Of course, as a wealthy woman herself, who could do what she wished, Marie was in a strong position to uphold the single state, but I suspect she would have loved receiving valentines, as she probably did from some of her more adoring fans. They were, after all, another form of attention, and Marie loved attention.

Although at the end of some of her novels and short stories her heroines did either die or marry (she couldn't entirely avoid the convention) in at least two stories the wives are overjoyed when the husband dies, and quite a few of her male characters end up dead (certainly not in the romantic tradition!). She was a writer of Romance, not a romantic writer, her books and stories are full of the outlandish and fantastical, but she was also a modernist who used all the latest scientific developments and theories to give weight to her plots. Marie loved talking to those with knowledge of such things, and though she had *The Dream*, her gondola, and ponies pulling a trap, she also had a brand new motor car.

Paper valentines had become so popular in England in the early 19th century that they were made in factories. Fancy valentines were made with real lace and ribbons, with paper lace introduced in the mid-19th century.

Marie carried on writing all her life and her last book, *Love and the Philosopher*, was published the year before her death. For all her engagement with the mores of her times, I think she stayed true to her first idealised vision of love as declared at the end of *Ardath*, (1889):

> Their love, their wondrous happiness, no mortal language can

define, for spiritual love perfected, as far exceeds material passion, as the steadfast glory of the sun outshines the flickering of an earthly taper.

Ponies, Trap and Marie Corelli
(photographed by Bertha Vyver)

APPENDIX F: Loyalists and Others

No-one exists in a vacuum, and Marie had her loyal band of friends, supporters and staff. After her death all the servants stayed on and the house was run as though she was still alive. Here are some of the key players in her life, both friendly and not so friendly.

Bertha Amelia Adriana Francisca Vyver, born 1854, was the second daughter of the Belgian Countess van der Vyver and Marie's lifelong friend and most loyal supporter. After Marie's death Bertha inherited the whole estate unconditionally and a trust fund was set up to run Mason Croft. However, a court decision was needed to ensure that Bertha was entitled to all money paid into Marie's account, including royalties. Bertha's *Memoirs of Marie Corelli* was published in 1930.

Arthur Bridges was Marie's butler, who aided and abetted Bertha in keeping the unwanted from their fragile charge. Anyone knocking on the door would have met this dignified and courteous man. After Marie's death, he was left two houses in Church Street, furniture, paintings, and a life position as custodian of Mason Croft.

Annie Davis had been a shorthand and typing teacher at the Technical School since 1895, and was also a stringer (part-time reporter) for the local paper when she became Marie's secretary in 1901, coping with her mountain of correspondence. She stayed with her for thirteen years, until family loyalty spelled the end of her employment. Annie subsequently ran a successful typing and shorthand school in Stratford for many years.

Frank Benson was a Shakespearian actor and frequent visitor, along with his wife, to Mason Croft. He ran the Shakespeare Festival for many years and was knighted in 1916.

Ellen Terry. A mutual admiration existed between her and Marie, and the celebrated actress supported Marie in her many conservation campaigns. In a career lasting almost 70 years, towards the end of the 19th century she was acclaimed as the leading

Shakespearean and comic actress in Britain. She died four years after Marie.

(Dr) Mary Scharlieb had trained in India before returning and completing her training at the Royal Free Hospital. She opened her own practice in Harley Street in 1887, when women doctors were scarce. She trained with Elizabeth Garrett Anderson and took over from her when she retired, as head of the New Hospital for Women. With a love of music in common, she and Marie were long-standing friends. Dr Scharlieb operated on Marie in 1897.

Thomas (Tommy) Lipton. Millionaire tea-magnate and yachtsman, he provided the sugar that led to Marie's conviction for sugar hoarding in 1918. He failed to win the Americas Cup five times, but lowered the price of tea for the middle and lower classes, and so is responsible for making Britain a tea-drinking nation! It was on board his yacht that the meeting occurred that saved Harvard House from dereliction. He was knighted by Queen Victoria in 1898.

William Wells Quatremain was a painter and frequent visitor at Mason Croft, who lived just up the road from Marie at 9 Church Street. Many of his paintings became postcards, and are still popular today as prints.

Sidney Lee. Shakespearean scholar, Chairman and Life Trustee of the SBT, his admiration for Marie's loyalty to the Bard was always tempered by his need to act in a certain way. He was knighted in 1911, and died two years after Marie.

Eric Mackay was Marie's stepbrother. While they were staying at the Falcon in 1889, Eric evidently read a guide book to the town [*Two Hours in Stratford-on-Avon*, 1889] written by the vicar of Holy Trinity Church, the Reverend George Arbuthnot, in which he wrote that Shakespeare was, 'we are sorry to say not a total abstainer.' Arbuthnot was a supporter of the temperance movement. Eric wrote to the local paper, the *Stratford-upon-Avon Herald*, challenging this opinion. In his letter, dated 29 May 1890, 'An Insult to Shakespeare', Eric Mackay argued that in the 16th century a man who did not drink was not considered a gentleman. This may say more about Mackay than about Shakespeare, as in Tudor times everyone, including children, drank alcohol due to the dangerous quality of the water. He started the letter, 'In a flippant little guide-book entitled "Two Hours in Stratford-on-Avon," I read with amazement, not unmixed with pity for the writer of such stuff the following remarks regarding the immortal Shakespeare' and ended the letter that he thought this was, 'a gratuitous insult to the Poet's memory... Surely a man in his position should have known better?' He also regarded the notion that the young William might have merited punishment at the hands of his teacher, 'a trumpery idea.'

Fred Winter. By the outbreak of the First World War, Fred Winter had the lease on 14, 16, 17 and 18 High Street, and in 1917, with the addition of numbers 30 & 31, dominated both sides of the road. As well as a successful businessman, Fred was mayor of Stratford-upon-Avon for two years running, in 1913-14 and 1914-15; he was also a JP and Alderman, and in the early 1930s became Master of his local Freemason's Lodge.

There's still a Fred Winter presence in town. No. 8 Henley Street now carries on the family tradition, just a few doors away from the public library.

George Boyden was the Editor of the *Stratford-upon-Avon Herald*. The paper began life in 1860 and was taken over by the Boyden family in 1880; it is still a family-run business today. Marie sued George Boyden for libel, later withdrawn, when he published an editorial suggesting that Marie's opposition to the Free Library was because it was to be a Carnegie, not Corelli, library.

Marie Corelli: Shakespeare's Champion

APPENDIX G: Map: places of interest

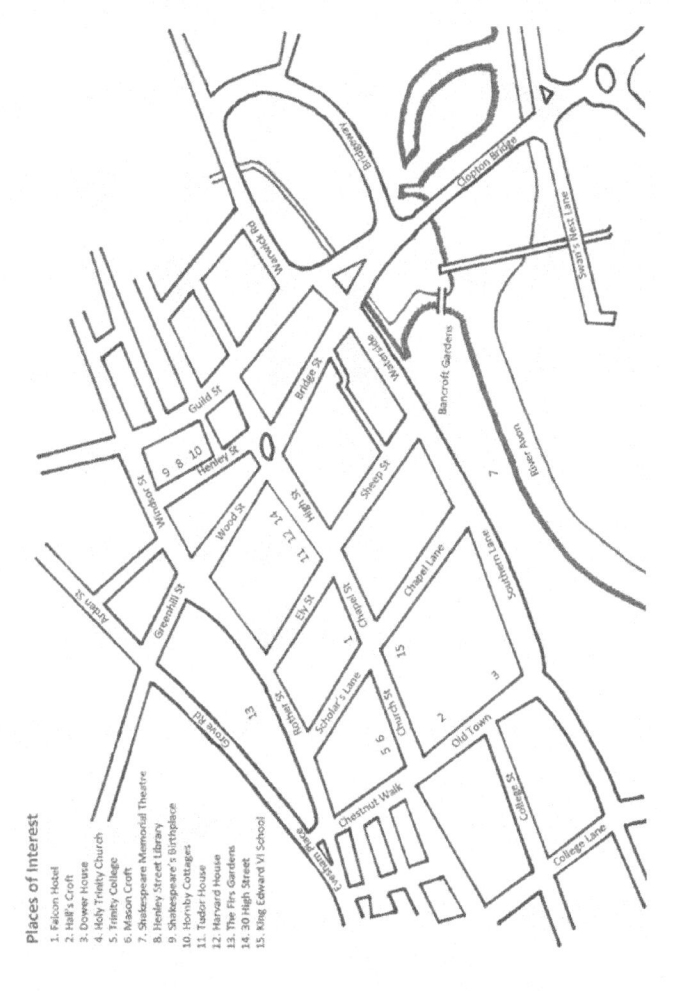

Places of Interest

1. Falcon Hotel
2. Hall's Croft
3. Dower House
4. Holy Trinity Church
5. Trinity College
6. Mason Croft
7. Shakespeare Memorial Theatre
8. Henley Street Library
9. Shakespeare's Birthplace
10. Hornby Cottages
11. Tudor House
12. Harvard House
13. The Firs Gardens
14. 30 High Street
15. King Edward VI School

ACKNOWLEDGEMENTS

This book could not have been written without the help and encouragement of a number of people.

Thanks are due to Katherine McMaster and Bren Littlewood, my beta readers, for their insightful and much valued comments. Bren writes crime fiction as JJ Franklin: https://www.bmlittlewood.com

Also to the Shakespeare Birthplace Trust, and Jennifer Jones, for access to and use of the photographs in the collection.

To all those responsible for the restoration of Marie's grave angel.

Mostly, my thanks are due to Ellie Stevenson (https://www.amazon.co.uk/Ellie-Stevenson/e/B007UF15I4), who coached me and finally shifted the blocks that were stalling my completion of the project.

Thank you one and all.

Marie Corelli Memorial Grave with Restored Angel, 2017
(photography by Ellie Stevenson)

SOURCES AND BACKGROUND READING

Bearman, R. 1988. *Stratford-upon-Avon: A History of its Streets and Buildings*. Lancashire: Hendon Publishing Co Ltd

Bell, Maureen. 2011. *Mason Croft*: Leaflet: A Brief History

Bloom, James Harvey, (ed). 1903. *The Errors of the Avon Star. Another Literary Manual for the Stratford-on-Avon Season of 1903. [On "The Avon Star" by Marie Corelli]*. Stratford-upon-Avon

Burley, Paul, and Robert Bearman. 2013. Leaflet: *the frieze*. Stratford-upon-Avon: Stratford-upon-Avon Society

Catalogue of an Exhibition of Books, Manuscripts, Letters, Photographs, & other items relating to Marie Corelli in her former home, Mason Croft, Stratford-upon-Avon, now the Shakespeare Institute. 1964. Stratford-upon-Avon: Shakespeare Institute

Corelli, Marie, (ed). *1903. The Avon Star: A literary manual for the Stratford-on-Avon season of 1903, April 23rd*. Stratford-on-Avon: AJ Stanley, Tudor House

Corelli, Marie. 1903. *The Plain Truth of the Stratford-on-Avon Controversy concerning the fully-intended demolition of old houses in Henley Street, and the changes proposed to be effected on the National Ground of Shakespeare's Birthplace*. London: Methuen & Co [Reproduced by Nabu Press in 2010, as being culturally important]

Corelli, Marie. 1916. *Shakespeare at School. Address to the boys of the Stratford-on-Avon Grammar School, on the Tercentenary of Shakespeare's death, May II, MCMXVI*. London: Geo W Jones

Corelli, Marie. 1916. *With Shakespeare in his Garden. An Invitation to the Summer Festival at Stratford-upon-Avon from July 29 to August 26 1916*. Taunton: The Wessex Press

Corelli, Marie (preface). 1916. *Messages of Sympathy and Consolation to The World in Tears*. London: Robert Hayes

Corelli, Marie. 1916. *A "happy thoughts" Day. Written specially for the Grantham Red Cross Outings Fund*

Corelli, Marie, Percy S Brentnall, Bertha Vyver. 1929. *Harvard House Stratford-upon-Avon Guide Book compiled and edited Under authority of the Harvard House Memorial Trustees [1909]*

Corelli, Marie. 1919. My Little Bit. Inspirational Essays on Current Topics. New York: George H Doran

Federico, Annette R. 2000. *Idol of Suburbia: Marie Corelli and Late-Victorian Literary Culture*. Virginia: University Press of Virginia

Fogg, Nicholas. 2014. *Stratford-upon-Avon The Biography: The history of the city through the voices of Stratford-upon-Avon's inhabitants, from its earliest origins to the present.* Gloucestershire: Amberley Publishing

Fogg, Nicholas (ed). 1990. *Victorian Stratford-upon-Avon in Old Photographs, from the collections of the Shakespeare Birthplace Trust*. Gloucestershire: Alan Sutton Publishing

Forrest, H.E. 1925. *The Old Houses of Stratford-upon-Avon*. London: Methuen

Knowles, James. *The Corelli Papers*. Quarterly broadsheet distributed and written by James Knowles between 1964 and 1968

1974. 'Stratford's Other Scribe - Marie Corelli'. *The Lady*

Lee, Sidney. *1903. The Alleged Vandalism at Stratford-on-Avon*. Westminster: Constable

Margesson, Frances. 1968. *Late and Soon*. London: John Murray

http://mariecorelli.org.uk/ - interesting website for Corelli fans [Accessed 18/05/2017]

Oldfield, John D, (ed). 1996. The Archive Photographs Series, *Stratford-upon-Avon and Beyond*, compiled by John D Oldfield. Gloucestershire: The Chalford Publishing Company

Ransom, Teresa. 1999. *The Mysterious Miss Marie Corelli: Queen of Victorian Bestsellers*. Gloucestershire: Sutton Publishing Limited

Scott, Enid Stuart. 1972. *The Magnificent Marie*. Unpublished manuscript

Scott, William Stuart. 1955. *Marie Corelli: the story of a friendship*. London: Hutchinson

Stevenson, Ellie. 2013. *Fascinating Ladies: Marie Corelli*. Available at
http://henpicked.net/stratford-upon-avons-other-writer-marie-corelli/
[Accessed 21/07/2015] Note: the title was changed from the original *Stratford-upon-Avon's Other Writer: Marie Corelli*

The Stratford-upon-Avon Canal Society. Summer 2011. *Newsletter*. Issue 351

Strong, Roy. 2016. *The Quest for Shakespeare's Garden*. London: Thames & Hudson Ltd

Thomas, Julia. 2012. *Shakespeare's Shrine: The Bard's Birthplace and the Invention of Stratford-upon-Avon.* Pennsylvania: University of Pennsylvania Press

Vyver, Bertha. 1930. *Memoirs of Marie Corelli*. London: Alston Rivers Ltd

INDEX

Alveston Leys 52
Anderson, Mary 52
Arbuthnot, Rev George 14, 44, 128
Bancroft Basin 16, 19, 108
Benson, Frank 126
Bentley, George 95, 99, 105
Bentley, Richard 99
Birch's china shop 24, 26, 31
Birmingham newspapers 15. 29
Bloom, Harvey 67, 108, 109
    work: *Errors of the Avon Star* 67, 108
Boyden, George 10, 66, 71, 130
Bridges, Arthur 125
British Archaeological Association 26
British Red Cross Society 52, 56
Carnegie, Andrew 24-25, 28, 29
Corelli, Marie, novels:
    Ardath 97, 122
    Barabbas 100, 106
    Boy 55
    God's Good Man 67, 109
    Life Everlasting, The 73
    Love and the Philosopher 111, 122
    Mighty Atom, The 101
    Romance of Two Worlds, A 72, 95-96, 105
    Secret Power, The 74-75, 111

  Sorrows of Satan, The 60, 100-101, 106
  Soul of Lilith, The 98, 106
  Thelma 97, 105
  Vendetta 97, 105
  Wormwood 98, 106
  Young Diana, The 111, 120
Corelli, Marie, other works:
  Avon Star, The 20, 67, 108
  "happy thoughts" Day, A 60
  My Little Bit 62
  Shakespeare at School 58
  With Shakespeare in his Garden 43, 60, 61
  World in Tears, The 56-57
Croker, Catherine 7, 107, 115
Davis, Annie 47, 69, 107, 126
Dickens, Charles 1
Docker, Ludford 52
Falcon Hotel 7, 98, 105, 128
Farthing Fund, The 69
Faucit, Helen 13
Firs, The and the Firs Gardens 44-45, 82, 110
Food hoarding 70-71
Free Public library, The 24, 26, 68, 108, 130
Gondola (*The Dream*) 69, 109, 122
Hall's Croft 7, 107, 115-116
Harvard House 35, 37-38, 41, 44, 109, 110, 127
Harvard House Guide Book 37, 38-39
Harvard, John 35-36, 39

Henley Street 23-24, 28, 30, 62, 67, 68, 83, 108, 113
Holy Trinity Church 8, 12, 13, 44, 47, 107, 110
Hornby Cottages 28, 30, 31
King Edward VI School (KES) 58
Labouchere, Henry 99
Lee, Sir Sidney 16, 59, 82, 109, 128
Leggett, Betty 115-117
Lipton, Sir Thomas (Tommy) 36, 40, 52, 70, 109, 127
Mackay, Charles 91-92, 94, 97, 103, 104, 105
Mackay, Elizabeth Mary (Ellen Mills) 91, 92, 93, 103, 104
Mackay, Eric 7, 94, 98, 99, 101, 102, 104, 105, 107, 128
Mackay, Minnie 91, 92, 93-94, 98, 103-104, 105
Margesson, Frances 115-116
Martin, Sir Theodore 13-14
Mason Croft 8, 11, 38, 62, 67, 70-71, 81-82, 86, 107, 125, 126, 128
Methuen 100
Morris, Edward 37, 38, 39, 40, 109
New Place 41, 48
Ransom, Teresa 82, 100
    work: *Mysterious Miss Marie Corelli: Queen of Victorian Bestsellers, The* 10
Scharlieb, Dr Mary 101, 102, 127
Scott, Enid Stuart 51
    work: *Magnificent Marie, The* 51
Scott, William Stuart 73

Severn, Arthur 120
Shakespeare, Birthday celebrations 81
Shakespeare's Birthplace 23, 24, 28, 30, 113
Shakespeare's Birthplace Trust (SBT) 16, 26, 29, 41,
    45, 58, 59, 82, 83, 85, 116, 117, 128
Shakespeare's Grave 7, 14
Shakespeare Memorial Theatre 9, 10, 13, 15, 19
Shakespeare, William 2, 16, 26, 28-29, 30, 35, 94,
    115, 128, 129
Silver Domino, The (collection of essays) 99
Society for the Protection of Ancient Buildings 27
Stanley, AJ 44, 108
Stratford-upon-Avon Choral Union 10, 107
Stratford-upon-Avon Grammar School 9, 45, 58
Stratford-upon-Avon Herald 10, 11, 15, 20, 68, 81,
    108, 128, 130
Technical School 31, 32, 68, 126
Terry, Ellen 24, 25, 126
Trinity College 8, 62, 67, 108, 110, 111
Tudor House 44, 108
Vyver, Bertha 7, 8, 11, 36, 38, 44, 48, 52, 65, 71, 73
    82, 92, 93, 94, 97, 98, 101, 104, 105, 106, 107
    109, 125
    work: *Memoirs of Marie Corelli* 71, 73, 125
Walters, J Cuming 73
Wells, HG 1, 73, 96
Winter, Fred 48, 66, 68-69, 71, 108, 109, 110, 129
    130

Front cover image shows Marie Corelli at the wheel of Tommy Lipton's yacht, *Erin*, c1905

If you have memories, stories or photos of Marie Corelli you would like to share, the author would be delighted to hear from you.

Please email:

stratfordsmallhistories@gmail.com